MORE PICTURES
OF HEALTH

by

Cynthia O'Neill, S.R.N., S.C.M., Q.N., H.V.

Foreword by Professor June Clark, Ph.D., R.G.N., R.H.V., F.R.C.N.

Meadow Books
1991

Dedicated to all who serve the sick and suffering.

First published in 1991 by Meadow Books.

British Library Cataloguing in Publication Data
More Pictures of Health.
1. Great Britain. Nursing, history.
I. O'Neill, Cynthia
610.730941

ISBN 0-9515655-1-6

By the same author: 'A Picture of Health'

Printed and bound in Great Britain by Witley Press Ltd., 24 Greevegate, Hunstanton, Norfolk, PE36 6AD.

CONTENTS

ACKNOWLEDGEMENTS

The author wishes to thank the following for their valuable assistance:

M. H. Brooks for the loan of the postcard on page 46
Fulham and Hammersmith Libraries — cover
Glasgow Royal Infirmary — pages 57, 95 and 102
Glasgow Victoria Infirmary — page 42
P. Loobey — page 20
National Museum and Galleries of Merseyside — page 71
Nursing Archives of Australia (J.R.W.) Collection — pages 11, 76
Photocare Laboratories, Kingham — page 58
The Royal London Hospital Archives Centre — pages 60, 73
R. Stenlake — page 102
Trustees of the Imperial War Museum — pages 50, 51

Alexandra Rose Day Fund, Bedford General Hospital, Bolingbroke Hospital, Bristol Royal Infirmary
Chartered Society of Physiotherapy
Rebecca F. Cooper
Dyfed County Council (Lampeter Branch Library)
East Sussex County Libraries
Guy's Hospital
Miss E. James
Dorothy Jones
M. G. Mainwaring
Hugh McAurthur
Oxfordshire County Libraries
Queen Alexandra Royal Army Nursing Corps
Queen Alexandra Royal Naval Nursing Service
Royal Army Medical Corps Museum
Royal College of Nursing
Wellcome Museum of Medical Science
Miss E. White
Withington Hospital

Special thanks to the following for their financial assistance:

Britcair Ltd.
Convatec Limited
Hammersmith Hospital Nurses' League
Humanetics Medical Limited
Michael O'Neill
Royal College of Nursing
Royal College of Nursing, Scotland
Royal National Nurses' Pension Fund
Slumberland Medicare Ltd.
Spenco Med (UK) Ltd.
SSS Medical Services Ltd. Clinitron Therapy
Sterimatic Medical Systems Ltd.

Thanks are also due to the help received since this publication went to print.

Further Reading:
'British Nursing Badges' by Jennifer Meglaughlin (Published by Vade Mecum Press 1990)
'The Strange Story of Dr James Barry' by Isobel Rae (Published by Longmans, 1958)
'Four Years out of Life' by Lesley Smith (Published by Phillip Allen, 1931)

FOREWORD

This year, the Royal College of Nursing celebrates its 75th anniversary. It is an opportunity to reflect on past achievements and changing images of nursing as well as a chance to shape nursing's future.

'A Picture of Health', Cynthia O'Neill's first collection of picture postcards of nursing and hospitals, provided hours of gleeful nostalgia. I'm delighted therefore to see that she has succumbed to the pressure of many, many nurses, and produced a further instalment.

Flipping through the collection inevitably starts one speculating about the kind of pictures which would be representative of today's health services. Many of the buildings, of course, are still in use as most of our hospitals were built before the first world war. Inside, at first sight, they are less forbidding and the nursing staff perhaps a little less formidable.

Any 1990's picture collection would, of course, show many more people being cared for in their own homes and very few patients in the relaxed state of convalescence so beloved of the seaside naughty postcard. Yet some of the issues which consumed nurses' time and attention in the early years of the century are still with us. Fundraising for basic necessities as well as for extras, has made an unwelcome reappearance. At the less serious level, nurses still agonise about whether to discard their caps and uniforms but perhaps by the time we reach the third instalment of pictures, we will have buried our ''angel'' image once and for all?

Professor June Clark, Ph.D., R.G.N., R.H.V., F.R.C.N.
President, Royal College of Nursing

INTRODUCTION

Such has been the success of my first book 'A Picture of Health' both in Britain and abroad that many readers have written to me asking for a particular hospital or their old training school to be featured. In this second book I have included some Hospitals that did not appear in 'A Picture of Health'. If your Hospital is not shown and existed before 1910 then there are bound to be old picture postcards around, so please send me one. Perhaps even a third book?

As previously a small part of the proceeds will be sent to The Nation's Fund for Nurses (Reg. charity).

I am very happy that this new book will be published in the same year that The Royal College of Nursing now with over 290,000 members celebrates it's 75th birthday.

To those readers that have waited so patiently, here it is.

It is my earnest wish that these pages will record the dedication to duty, heroism and indeed self sacrifice shown by Nurses over the decades and it is certain that early Royal College of Nursing members are portrayed in this book.

Cynthia O'Neill,
22 Church Meadow,
Milton-under-Wychwood,
Oxford, OX7 6JG.
September, 1991.

"AND MATRON RULED LIKE A ROD OF IRON . . ."

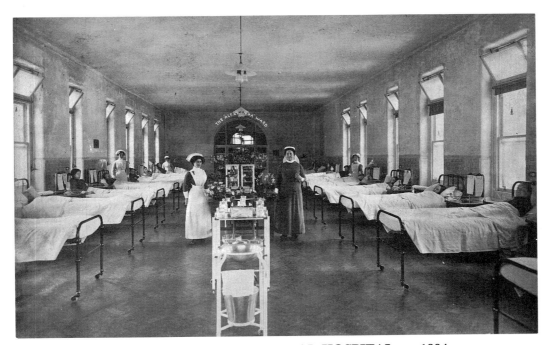

WOLVERHAMPTON GENERAL HOSPITAL, c. 1904

With every window open, all bed castor wheels turned inwards, floors shining like glass and patients neatly placed in beds the ward is hushed as Matron does her rounds. "This is Matron x Gertie" is the message. Notice the ward Sister to the front of the picture with her training school badge pinned to the right of her apron. These badges are now highly collectable treasures. This hospital has been replaced by The Royal Hospital and has 225 beds.

**YOURS SINCERELY,
J. LEADBETTER, MATRON,**
27.11.28
Who were these super human
creatures that reigned supreme as
Queens of our Hospitals? With soft
foot tread Matron glided into the
ward and in seconds the young
nurse could be reduced to tears.
What power she held! As Matron
walked, or sailed down the corridor
with this hat everyone vanished.
Does anyone know where this
gracious Matron reigned? Matrons
were not allowed to marry and at
all times had to be at the Hospital,
only having time off with the
permission from the Board of
Governors. Her whole life and
work was for the patients.

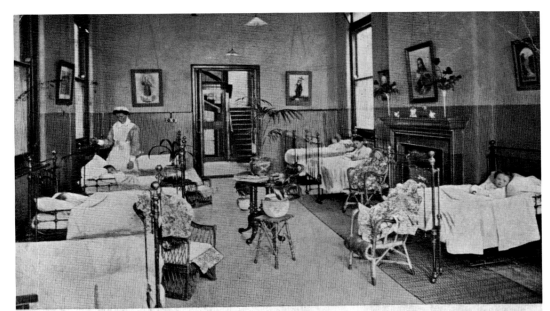

Mater Infirmorum Hospital, Belfast.   A Children's Ward.

MATER INFIRMORUM HOSPITAL, BELFAST, c. 1904
This wonderful Hospital founded in 1883 for the past few years has been treating seriously injured patients with gunshot wounds resulting from the sad conflict in Northern Ireland. It is a fact however that as a result of wars many notable advances in medicine and surgery have been made, for example Penicillin was developed and used in World War 2 saving countless lives.

BEDFORD GENERAL HOSPITAL, VICTORIA WARD, c. 1900
To amuse children during their often quite long stays in Hospital beautiful Doulton tiling adorned some of the walls. Look at Humpty Dumpty, Miss Muffit, Jack and Jill and Ride a cock horse as are the favourites here. Some of these tiles can still be seen as at Bedford General. Sadly in the name of progress many lovely, brightly coloured tiles have been smashed to pieces as modernisation takes place but the local children of Bedford are assured of a treat.

STAFF NURSE, c. 1904
(Unknown) Wimbledon
photographer

Nurses were so proud of their own
particular uniforms and caps.
Colours of the dresses varied from
grey, purple, green to pretty blue
and many different styles of caps
appeared. As the nurse worked her
way up the grand pecking order so
her cap became more elaborate.
Notice the bow or "strings" under
Staff Nurse's cap. Sister wears a
lace trimmed cap and the head
dress of a Matron was quite
unique! (see p. 2) A Probationer
(as she was called) would be
expected to buy yards of materials
to make or get made her dresses,
aprons, sleeves, cuffs, caps etc.
The badge worn shows a female
figure with a child held in her left
arm. Anyone recognize please?
Perhaps this badge is in a
collection?

5

"And Matron ruled like a rod of iron ..."

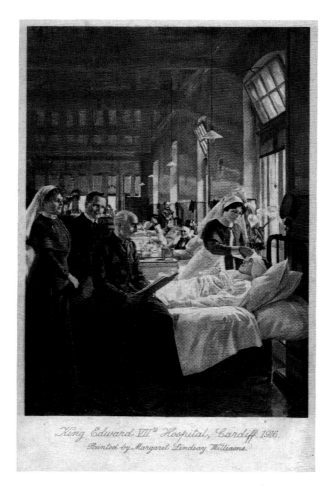

King Edward VIIᵗʰ Hospital, Cardiff. 1916.
Painted by Margaret Lindsay Williams.

KING EDWARD VII HOSPITAL, CARDIFF, 1916 This very striking original painting hangs in the entrance hall to the Cardiff Royal Infirmary (used to be King Edward VII Hospital). What old Hospital has not a ghost or two? A "grey lady" ghost is seen by terminally ill patients, nurses and others and is said to be the ghost of a Nurse killed in the course of duty. Asked to get a drink for a dying patient the Nurse dressed in the grey uniform of the day went to the lift door, opened it and fell down the shaft to her death.

WHAT WILL YOUR FUTURE BE? c. 1905

She would never become rich in money as the payment was so very low and sometimes nil but so rich of full and happy memories she could call upon in later life. These are qualified Nurses and as can be seen by their arm bands are District Nurses training to become Queen's Nursing Sisters to nurse the sick poor in their own homes.

A VERY LONG DAY

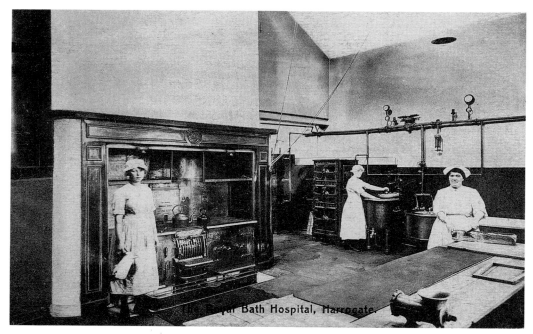

THE ROYAL BATH HOSPITAL, HARROGATE, c. 1910
The kitchens need to start early cooking for this 170 bedded Hospital that now cares for the elderly, those with rheumatic disease and the younger disabled. Notice the glorious old cooking range and assortment of pots, pans and kitchen equipment.
Our kitchen maid to the left looks very glum (see p. 19).

WITHINGTON GENERAL HOSPITAL, DIDSBURY, 1904-1912
Did these young nurses foresee how very large their little hospital would become now to have over 1,000 beds? Withington excels in the field of plastic surgery. Matron E. Smith R.R.C. brings her dog to be photographed too! Extensive enquiries fail to tell me if bows to the caps are Staff nurses. It appears that all Withington nurses even the most junior was awarded a bow. Someone thought all their nurses deserved such a frill as a bow at Withington!

LEICESTER ROYAL INFIRMARY X-RAY DEPT, c. 1905
With the discovery of X-rays in 1895 what a marvel it was to see the broken bones. Leicester Royal Infirmary was founded, ''for the sick poor of any county or nations'' (see Nursing Standard March 4th 1989, p. 34). A lovely homely Hospital. Compare this with today's modern facilities. Amy sends a message 19th May 1910 ''Dear Billy, I am sending you a card of the xrays this is what I went under Love to all Amy xxx''

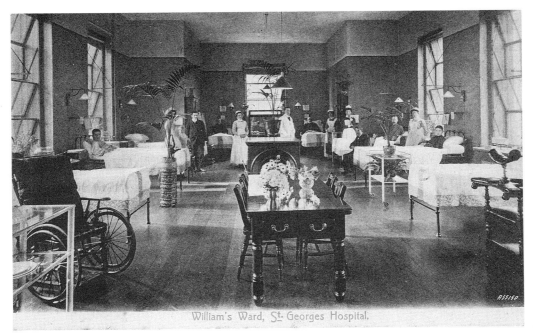

William's Ward, St. Georges Hospital.

WILLIAM'S WARD, ST. GEORGE'S HOSPITAL, HYDE PARK, c. 1906
Founded when this part of London was very quiet indeed to the noise, rush and hustle of the
nineties. St. George's with it's great tradition of first class service has now been refounded in
Tooting. The proud, strong, white handsome building of old St. George's is to be made
into an Hotel but thickly double glazed I hope!.

Royal Alexandra Hospital, Rhyl, N. Wales.   Laundry.

ROYAL ALEXANDRA HOSPITAL, RHYL LAUNDRY, 1908

One thing we all take for granted in the hospital: the clean linen. "To Charlotte, laundry maid 5/-", as a Christmas present from the Board of Governors. Frequently attached to the Hospital and responsible for the patient's linen and endless Nurses' aprons that may need fancy pleating after starching. Collars, caps and cuffs and Doctor's coats too would need starching. Caps were finished off and pressed by hand. Nowadays some Nurses prefer to wear mufti in place of the often uncomfortable, badly designed, poor fitting NHS regulation uniforms of the 90's though a few Hospitals keep their traditional uniforms (see p. 22).

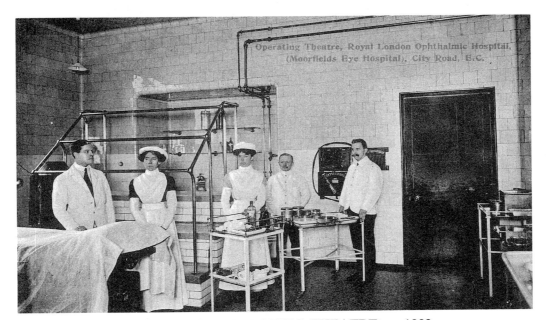

MOORFIELDS OPERATING THEATRE, c. 1902

The very first hospital in the world founded only for the treatment of patients with diseases of the eye, in 1805. Moorfields as we know today was built in 1898. What would the staff in this scene say if they could get a glimpse of an eye operation of the 90's and the delicate fine surgery? Just think of the engineers who design our fine instruments and equipment.

PRINCIPAL DISPENSING ROOM, ROYAL INFIRMARY, EDINBURGH.

INGLIS, PHOTOGRAPHER, EDINᴿ

PRINCIPAL DISPENSARY, ROYAL INFIRMARY, EDINBURGH, 1908
Ointments, pills, brightly coloured medicines, injections, kaolin and the famous mag. sulph.
paste lists a few of the items dispensed here daily for the wards, departments, casualty and
theatres. This card was a "begging card" and we learn from the report dated 1909
and to the back of the card —

New patients treated 11,566,   Outdoor patients treated 35,678   Av. daily in hospital 845
The report continues to say how much in debt they were i.e. £17,961 9s 11d. It was a wonder
how these hospitals kept going but they never closed (see p. 88).

BLIGHTY, 1915
Visiting was allowed but it was very restricted and even as recent as the early 60's it was two visitors a bed only and visiting cards to be shown. At the end of the precious half hour a bell is rung, "Time to go please visitors". This patient proves that being in a hospital bed does have some compensations. He is certainly enjoying his treats and all the fuss!

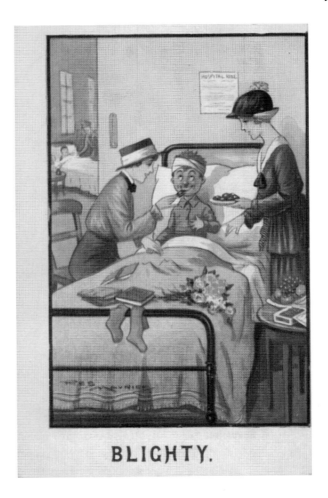

BLIGHTY.

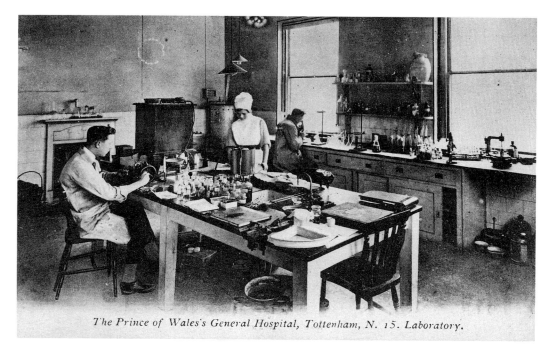

The Prince of Wales's General Hospital, Tottenham, N. 15. Laboratory.

PRINCE OF WALES GENERAL HOSPITAL, TOTTENHAM N.15, LONDON
A rare picture of an early hospital laboratory complete with coal fire and fresh buckets of coal. Well before the antibiotic age yet the microscopes are being put to good use. A large London hospital now non-existent. Pathologists and laboratory technicians provide too a round the clock service to the patient often working in a laboratory hidden away in a corner of the hospital or even underground. Their skilled frequently unseen work is much appreciated by all.

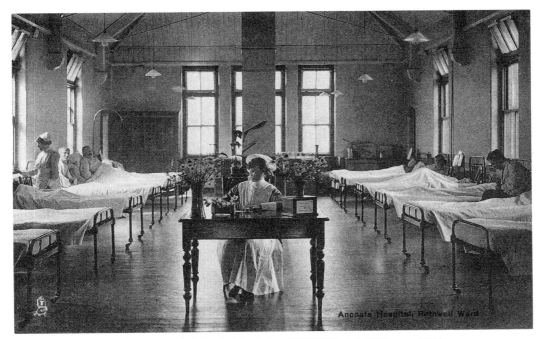

ANCOATS HOSPITAL, ROTHWELL WARD, c. 1902

All tucked up and ready for sleep as Sister writes her report. It has been a long day. Notice the alms box to the right of the picture. Some patients will have been cured, a few will have died and all will have received the love and care that only Ancoats can give and continues to give. ''May I never see in the patient anything but a fellow creature in pain''. From the oath and prayer of Maimonides 1135-1204.

KAOLIN AS A POULTICE WAS VERY SOOTHING

DR. BARNARDO'S HOMES.—SISTER EVA AND BLIND PERCY IN "HER MAJESTY'S" HOSPITAL FOR WAIF CHILDREN, STEPNEY CAUSEWAY, E.

SISTER EVA WITH BLIND BOY IN HER MAJESTY'S HOME FOR WAIF CHILDREN, STEPNEY CAUSEWAY

Perhaps the most important treatment of all any nurse can give to the patient is love and kindness. Today's high tech nursing is quite different to these scenes but a good nurse sees that nothing but the very best is good enough for the patient regardless of his/her nationality, colour, class, creed, friend or foe. Florence Nightingale reminded us what a great privilege it was for a nurse to care for the sick.

HARROGATE. ROYAL BATHS.

A HARROGATE HOT AIR ROOM

HARROGATE ROYAL HOSPITAL BATHS, A HARROGATE HOT AIR ROOM,
c. 1905

Similar to the sauna of today. Look at all the weird and mysterious electrical switches. Man has always known the beneficial effects of hot or cold to the tired, aching or diseased body and this soothing effect does in fact appear to go right through to the bone.

The patient is well cased in. Is he enjoying his treatment?

The message reads, ''No running away from it like Dad did'' (see p. 8).

19

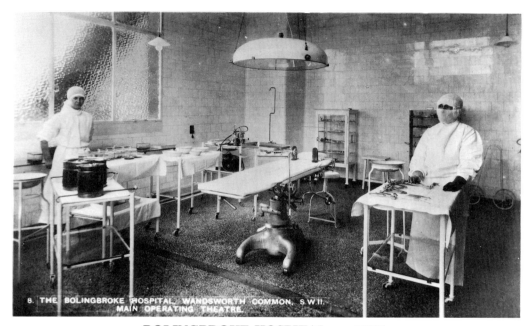

8. THE BOLINGBROKE HOSPITAL, WANDSWORTH COMMON, S.W.11.
MAIN OPERATING THEATRE.

BOLINGBROKE HOSPITAL, c. 1920's
A Bolingbroke should be in every town! Founded in 1880 in a quiet, poor corner of London and once a busy general hospital it now looks after the elderly sick of Wandsworth. Voted by "The Sunday Times" in 1989 as the Best Community Hospital. Win it again? See for yourself! The very active League of Friends are always providing much for the patients. Our founders and predecessors of Bolingbroke can look with pride upon their prize winner.
(Courtesy from the collection of P. Loobey)

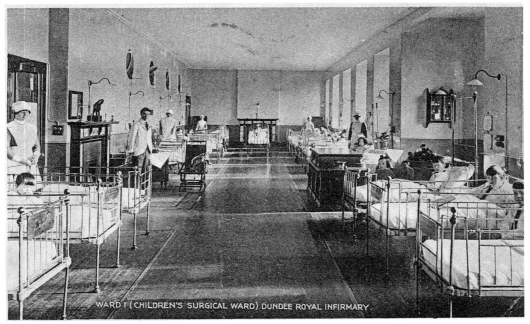

WARD I (CHILDREN'S SURGICAL WARD) DUNDEE ROYAL INFIRMARY.

WARD I, CHILDREN'S SURGICAL, DUNDEE ROYAL INFIRMARY, 1905
A great change of scene from the ward of 1991. Not a parent or toy in sight. Each cot has a
plaque with the name of the kind donor. The removal of tonsils was a fashionable operation at
this time. The children did like the ice cream given at frequent intervals as a
necessary part of their treatment.

Royal Alexandra Hospital. Rhyl. Salt-Water Bath.

ROYAL ALEXANDRA HOSPITAL, RHYL, SALT WATER BATH, c. 1904
Early hydrotherapy but I wonder how warm the water is? So many movements can be done in
the water with the minimum of effort and these exercises on dry land may be impossible. Who
in the long dresses would wade in should one of these little patients get into difficulty? This
disused pool now lies resting like a hallowed tomb as the Alex above continues in it's
unbroken tradition of service since 1872 (see p. 12).

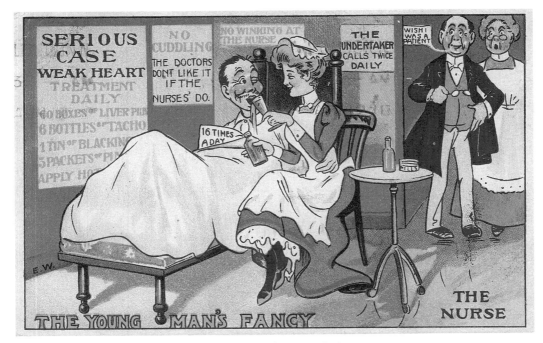

THE NURSE, c. 1910
"Don't make me laugh nurse or I'll burst my stitches." Often heard on the surgical wards. Laughter they say is the best medicine. A nurse needs so many skills and frequently has to cheer a patient up. "There is not one job you will not be expected to do as a nurse". How right this saying was as no two days of a nurse's life are ever the same.

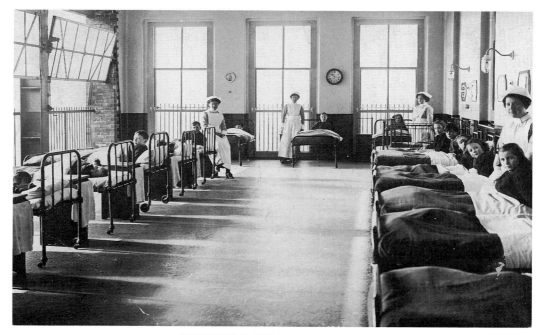

HESWALL HOSPITAL, 1912

When fresh air was high on the treatment list and ozone was a cure for all! These children suffering from diseases of the chest are strictly placed boys on one side and girls on the other. Matron will *not* be pleased when she sees nurse to the left of picture leaning against the bed but this was a specially posed "Watch the birdie" photograph.

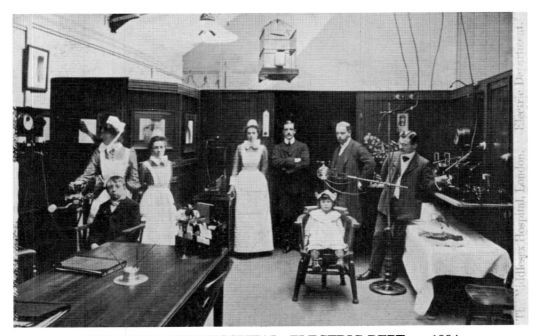

THE MIDDLESEX HOSPITAL, ELECTRIC DEPT, c. 1904

Is that a bird cage suspended from the ceiling? Look closely and indeed it is. Perhaps a budgie would sing and amuse the patients? This picture appears to show early electrical therapy treatment. Today's Physiotherapists can be seen in and out of any hospital ward and they too use electricity in some treatments. A long extensive training is needed to become a Physiotherapist or a ''Physio'' but he or she will get those mended bones moving properly.

Men's Surgical Ward — Cheltenham General Hospital

CHELTENHAM GENERAL HOSPITAL, MEN'S SURGICAL WARD, c. 1904
Pin pricks to the centre of the card denotes that someone had actually pinned this card to a wall. A momento of their operation or is Aunt Matilda in the scene? "Diseases desperate grown by desperate appliances are relieved or none at all", said Shakespeare. The dripping Chloroform was not a pleasant procedure then neither was the piece of cork placed in a patient's mouth to bite on and suffer! The Royal London Hospital still has the famous operation bell that would ring and summon attendants to hold down the poor victim about to be operated on. A grim reminder.

THE LOCAL COTTAGE HOSPITAL OR THE INFIRMARY?

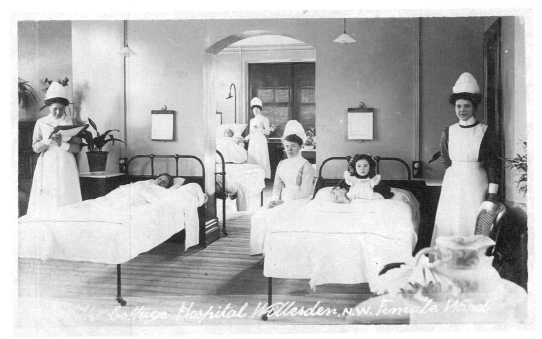

THE COTTAGE HOSPITAL, WILLESDEN N.W., FEMALE WARD, c. 1903

Cottage hospitals were small and friendly local hospitals, the idea being that some patients would prefer being cared for locally than in the large cities. What a superb picture so full of action. The young patient to the right has brought in her doll to play with. Still standing this little hospital now serves the chronic and elderly sick.

CROWTHER VAD HOSPITAL, SOUTHBOROUGH, KENT, 1917
Neither Cottage nor Infirmary but a canvas tent in the open air. Other WWI hospitals were set up in churches, village halls, schools and stately homes. Local people were known to give so much to equip these hospitals from crockery to blankets and of course personal unpaid service.

A LIVERPOOL PHOTOGRAPHER, 1914

Just look at those lovely hats and see the scissors tucked into their belts. These nurses are wearing a check material dress. What are the toys doing? Today's nurse has her scissors attached to a chain as these items so frequently go walkies; mine were always getting lost. In her short coffee break each morning the nurse says ''Please may I be excused'', and then has to make her bed and properly too and change into a clean apron and very quickly drink her coffee.

NURSE ETHEL HINES, SBM,
c. 1918
Her nursing skills were always in demand as she would be needed in foreign lands many miles away from her training school. Working in a hot, sticky desert to the icy polar region in often very difficult conditions, it is the nurse's job to bring health and healing to those she serves.

SBM MISSIONARY GROUP, SENDAMANGALA, c. 1918
Nurse Hines is seen seated first right of picture amongst her patients. Nurses were often sent out to the mission field attached to a particular church or religious community. Missionary nurses have been savagely murdered in the course of their duty or died from diseases such as leprosy. Today's great missionary nurse and inspiration to us all is Mother Teresa of Calcutta.

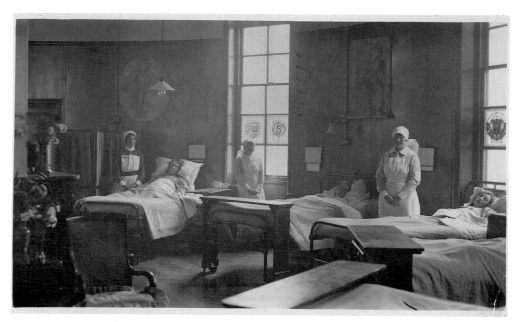

**ELIZABETH GARRET ANDERSON HOSPITAL,
WESTLAKE SURGICAL WARD,** c. 1923
For years now this hospital has provided a wonderful service to the women of London.
Founded in 1866 by Dr Elizabeth Garret Anderson. These stained glass windows remain in
place today. Over recent years the powers that be have sought so hard to dispose of this fine
little hospital but win they cannot! EGA stands for too much. It will never die or allow itself
to be bulldozed over.

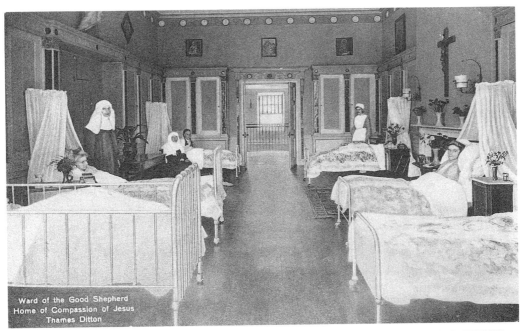

Ward of the Good Shepherd
Home of Compassion of Jesus
Thames Ditton

WARD OF THE GOOD SHEPHERD, HOME OF COMPASSION OF JESUS, THAMES DITTON, c. 1920

What cosy looking beds in this Cottage Hospital that had it's own small operating theatre. It was so often nuns that would choose to care for the incurable, dying and hopeless patients that the hospitals could do no more for. Now demolished and only a memory.

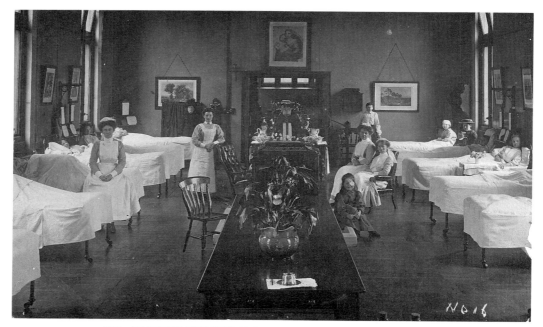

ST. JAMES' HOSPITAL, LEEDS, WARD XVI, 1908

Affectionately known as ''Jimmies'', the largest teaching hospital in Europe with 1395 beds, made famous by the popular television series in the 90's and a new showing in 1991. XVI is an Eye ward. Who are the ladies, one standing in front of a screen, the other seated? Are they lady visitors appointed by the Board of Governors whose job it was to visit the wards to see that all was in order and then to write a report to Matron?

ALWAYS LEARNING

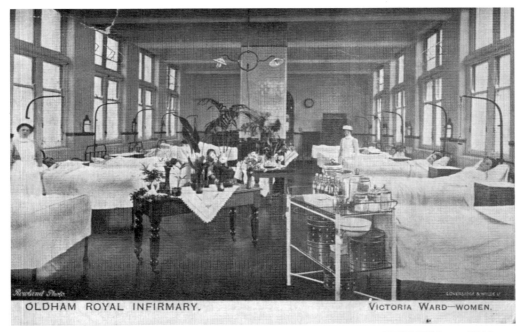

OLDHAM ROYAL INFIRMARY.   VICTORIA WARD—WOMEN.

OLDHAM ROYAL INFIRMARY, VICTORIA WARD, WOMEN, c. 1910

What a lot to learn for any young nurse apart from hospital etiquette. Trays and trolleys (see right of picture) needed laying up for various treatments and procedures. The stainless steel round large tins known as drums were filled with cotton wool balls and dressings and sterilized by autoclaving. Steam would penetrate through the holes in the drums that were moved open. In this throw away age dressings etc. all come pre packed and dressing forceps in fact are disposable. These drums have long since been scrapped.

A busy acute hospital of 160 beds.

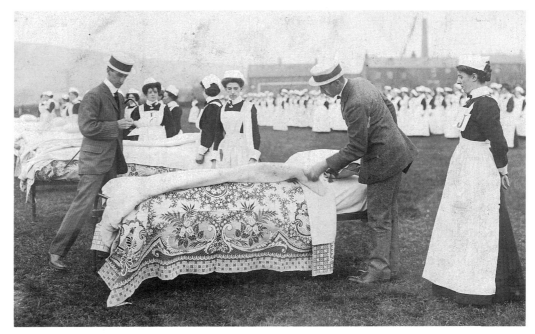

BED MAKING COMPETITION, c. 1908

Beds, beds and more beds to make. All beds were completely stripped and remade at least twice a day so one needed to be very quick to get all the many other ward jobs done. It was a race against time every day as the ward clock ticked away. Where is this great gathering of nurses? How many entrants and what is the prize? Will N.J. to the right of picture be the fastest bed maker?

SINCERELY YOURS, SISTER MINNIE

Responsible for the ward at all times even when off duty. At some hospitals sister's bed sitting room was attached to the ward! A very well respected lady of the hospital.

On wards of Leicester Royal Infirmary one can today see the little room above the ward that was where the Sister would sleep at night but I am sure Sister was many a night up nursing her patients.

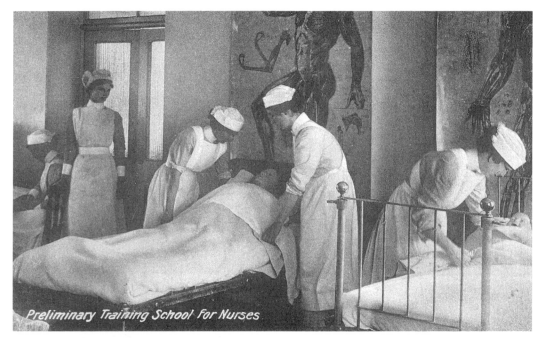

Preliminary Training School for Nurses

PRELIMINARY TRAINING SCHOOL, ST. THOMAS' HOSPITAL, LONDON, c. 1922
The famous hospital at which Florence Nightingale chose to found the Nightingale training
school for nurses. Basic introduction in anatomy, physiology, hygiene, bandaging, bed
making, and nursing procedures were the order of the day not to mention sick room cookery.
How many new nurses were brought to tears when the junket turned out to be anything else
but a junket? ''That will never do nurse.'' Following an examination pass the
nurse then proudly is allotted her first ward.

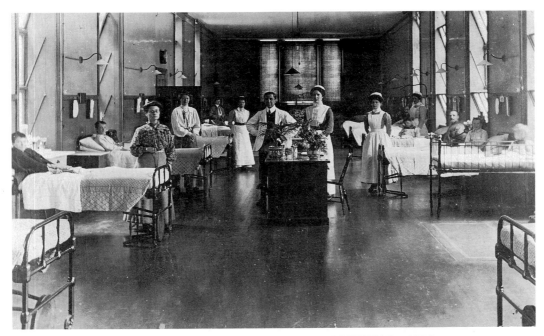

MOORE WARD, ROYAL FREE HOSPITAL, 1903
Used to be the only hospital offering training to women doctors. The entrance hall contains a
fantastic mural depicting the history of the Royal Free. Founded by William Marsden in 1828
who found a female under eighteen years of age, lying on the steps of St Andrew's
churchyard Holborn hill, after midnight actually perishing from disease and famine. The
school of nursing started in 1889 and Matron for that year earned £41. Today the Royal Free
is situated in a pleasant new building in Hampstead.

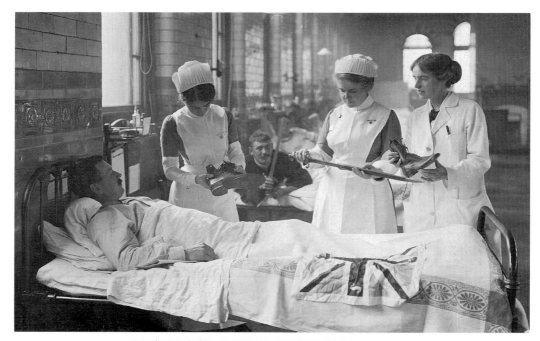

LIVERPOOL ROYAL INFIRMARY, c. 1916

What a lovely well made shoe and will it fit? There are so very many other ancillary workers attached to any hospital. Here the Almoner is admiring a boot made by the Surgical boot fitter. The patient is more interested in the German sword he captured from the battlefield. This beautiful old red brick building stands empty and desolate as weeds grow up the walls and birds fly in and out of the wards. Opposite the new Liverpool Royal Infirmary keeps watch. No one can bring themself to sign away the old Infirmary's death warrant.

THE OUT-PATIENTS' WAITING HALL. Thompson & Lee, Photo, N/C.
Royal Victoria Infirmary, Newcastle-upon-Tyne.

**OUT PATIENTS DEPT, ROYAL VICTORIA INFIRMARY,
NEWCASTLE ON TYNE,** 1904

Look at the serious expressions on their faces and at the queue going out of the door even.
For hours they have been waiting to be seen. In those days the Consultants all gave their time
to the Infirmary or Hospital on a voluntary basis. I like the assortment of hats.

41

ROYAL VICTORIA INFIRMARY, SCOTLAND, c. 1920
All very attentive and listening to sister's words of wisdom. Nurses had to attend a certain number of lectures both in their on and off duty time and even if this entailed rising from a warm bed sleeping after night duty the lectures were not to be missed. Notice the anatomical model with removable bits in the case. The author as a young student nurse hated these horrid things and they gave her bad dreams. Hardly surprising?
(Courtesy of Royal Victoria Infirmary, Scotland)

"MONEY, PLEASE..."

HOSPITAL FOR SICK CHILDREN, GT. ORMOND ST, MR. PUNCH'S COT, 1900

The cost of subscribing to a cot or bed varied from hospital to hospital but £100 was often the price of a cot in 1900 and a great deal of money. Who was Mr. Punch? Brass plates above beds or cots in some wards of our older hospitals still can be seen today and are lovingly polished as the name of the kind benefactor gleams in the sunshine. The new Charing Cross hospital in London has carefully placed the old brass plates removed from the beds of the original Charing Cross hospital so that they can now be admired in the entrance hall.

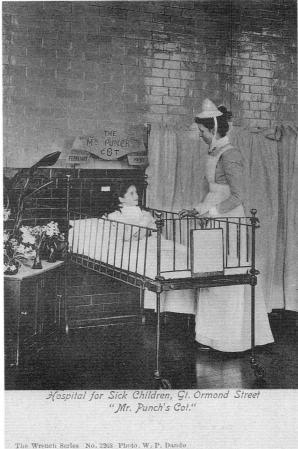

Hospital for Sick Children, Gt. Ormond Street
"Mr. Punch's Cot."

The Wrench Series No. 2263 Photo. W. P. Dando

43

ALEXANDRA ROSE DAY, 1917

Founded in 1912 as the very first Flag Day the aim being to help the sick and disabled and organisations caring for them. Now after seventy nine flag days the charity covers many charities that in 1912 were non existent. The charity one collects for can keep 80% of money raised. As a young District Nurse the author was duly handed a box of pink roses and a collecting tin and expected to take the box on her rounds. Some money did go in the tin, a few roses vanished but the money was not from the very poor patients of her district!

BIRKENHEADS HOSPITAL, c. 1903

Few if any hospitals were ever free from debt and they all always were entirely dependent upon the generosity and kindness of patients, visitors and the local community but everyone gave according to their means. Home made jams, eggs, a few pound notes, sheets, crockery to office writing paper. You will see such gifts listed in any Minutes books of your old hospital. Notice the collecting tin in full view and behind that a box for Christmas decorations. All that remains of this hospital today is a fond memory.

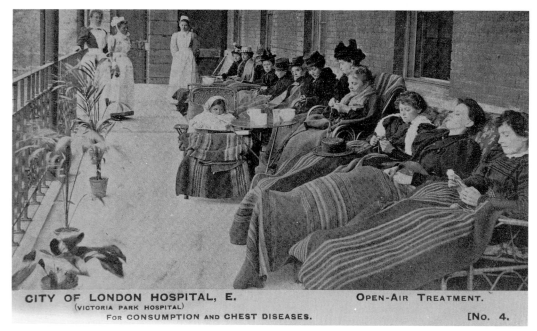

CITY OF LONDON HOSPITAL, E.
(VICTORIA PARK HOSPITAL)
FOR CONSUMPTION AND CHEST DISEASES.

OPEN-AIR TREATMENT.

[No. 4.

CITY OF LONDON HOSPITAL, E. (VICTORIA PARK HOSPITAL) FOR CONSUMPTION AND CHEST DISEASES, OPEN AIR TREATMENT

"Thank you for the gift of 1lb of silver paper." I wonder what that was worth? How thoughtful of the hospital to write to thank the donor for really so small a gift. This shows the treatment of the day. Notice how well clad the patients are and wrapped up in blankets. Some patients even slept at night in the open air.
(From the collection of Melwyn H. Brooks, Karkhur, Israel)

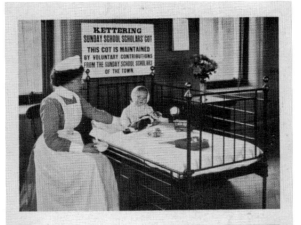

SUNDAY SCHOOL SCHOLAR'S COT, KETTERING & DISTRICT GENERAL HOSPITAL, c. 1904

What does the 1991 children's ward of this hospital of 554 beds look like. Perhaps the lovely old brass plaque over the cot remains? I doubt it. Certainly the cost of maintaining a cot far exceeds £30 a year today!

Sunday School Scholar's Cot

KETTERING & DISTRICT GENERAL HOSPITAL

¶ Contributions for this Cot will be received by your teacher next Sunday, and it is hoped that every scholar will give something. The amount required to maintain the Cot is £30 a year.

SPEIGHT, PHOTO., KETTERING.

"KILLED, DIED OF WOUNDS, REPORTED MISSING..."

Dames ambulancières Anglaises installant leur tente | English lady nurses getting their tents ready

ENGLISH LADY NURSES GETTING THEIR TENTS READY, c. 1914
Yes sadly nurses did die on war service. QARANC lost a total of 195 nurses in WWI. The Royal Navy also had nurses who gave the supreme sacrifice. Nurses were tortured by the enemy, drowned and some were torpedoed. A retired QA (Army nursing sister) now well in her late eighties said, ''It was a lucky job I was a Girl Guide as I was the only one that could pitch the tent''. The speed at which a complete tented hospital could be got ready was quite remarkable.

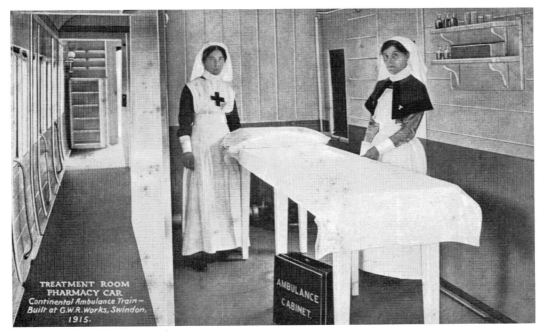

TREATMENT ROOM
PHARMACY CAR
Continental Ambulance Train –
Built at G.W.R. Works, Swindon,
1915.

AMBULANCE
CABINET.

TREATMENT ROOM, PHARMACY CAR, CONTINENTAL AMBULANCE TRAIN, 1915

Wounded from the war zones, the patient would know that he will always get the best of care from his nurses. With skilled attention the injured serviceman is transferred by ship or train to the hospitals at home or "Blighty". These very seriously ill patients would need treatments, e.g. dressings, done on the possibly long train journeys.

VOLUNTEER NURSES, FANYS GET THEIR AMBULANCES READY, c. 1917
Founded in 1907 as the First Aid Nursing Yeomanry (FANY) and now known as the
Women's Transport Service. In WW2 many Fanys served in the SOE. A Fany was often seen
as a driver of an ambulance taking the wounded from the casualty clearing stations to the
hospitals. With the men on the battlefield it was up to these girls to mend
and repair the ambulance.
(Courtesy of the Trustees, Imperial War Museum)

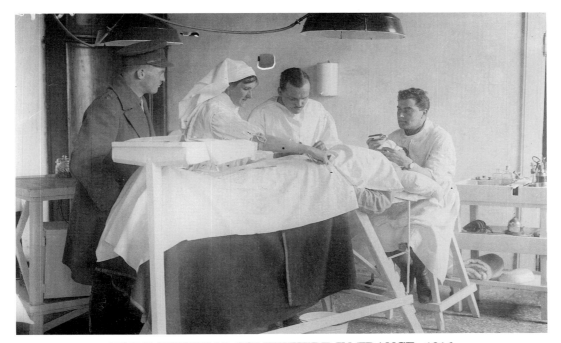

FIELD HOSPITAL SOMEWHERE IN FRANCE, 1916
An Anaesthetist slowly drops sleep inducing Chloroform to the face mask on the wounded soldier. Operating theatres were set up with incredible speed as surgeons, nurses and others worked hours non stop to alleviate the suffering and distress often against the noise of bombing and fire. Stretcher bearers would continually bring in those needing care. Many stories have been written in praise of these heroic teams (see suggested reading). Due to the shortage of Anaesthetists during WWI some QA's were taught to give anaesthetics.
(Courtesy of the Trustees, Imperial War Museum)

51

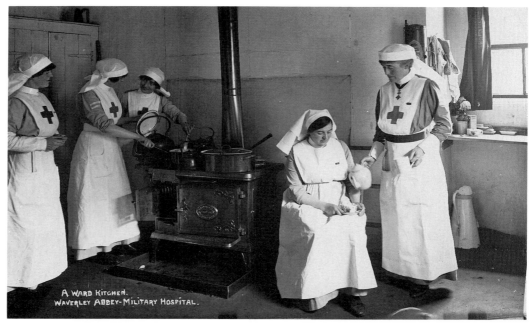

A WARD KITCHEN WAVERLEY ABBEY MILITARY HOSPITAL, c. 1918
Tea again but always so extra nice behind the kitchen door with Matron or Sister on the war
path! This picture shows our unpaid nurses, the VADS, wearing the Red Cross on their
aprons. Seated but wearing a different form of head dress this could be a Staff nurse or a
Sister. They had all worked hard and deserved a tea break, because on busy days
tea times could disappear.

WARD 7, GROUND FLOOR, DUSTON, 1918

A typical scene in a WWI hospital although in many pictures you will see the beds put closer together as more casualties returned. The message reads, "This is the ward in which I was in at Northampton and a jolly good hospital. I have marked x over the bed I was in I think you will see it from yours old Pal Jim". Well done Duston!

NURSE ELLA RICHARDS OF LAMPETER DYFED WALES, RED CROSS VAD

The wording on the memorial plaque at Soar Congregational Chapel Lampeter reads —
"In loving memory of
Nurse Ella Richards VAD.
Ardwyr, Bridge St., Lampeter
who died of pneumonia in Salonika
on Oct 14th 1918 aged 31 years.
She was buried in MIKRA
CEMETARY
SALONIKA,
For 3½ years she gave
dedicated service to
The Red Cross Nursing Society.
She has done what she could."
This plaque was given by her
"Sunday school class".

TO THE MEMORY OF NURSE RICHARDS WHO DIED IN THE GREAT WAR 1914-1919

Nurse Ella Richards was the daughter of the late Mr and Mrs Timothy Richards and the family consisted of two sons and three daughters. Mr Timothy Richards JP and his wife were held in high esteem in the town and people today still remember them. Due to intense cold of the tented hospitals in France Ella would wear strong boots, a sweater and on top of that an Officer's "British warm" over her uniform. When going from wards she carried a hurricane lamp. What more could this Nurse have done?

fêtes de la Victoire à Londres
Défilé des nurses

J·F

FETES DE LA VICTOIRE A LONDRES DEFILE DES NURSES, 1919

After the battle comes the victory but every battle has a high price to pay. The Nurses War Memorial chapel in Westminster Abbey contains a casket with the names of no less than 3,076 men and women who lost their lives in service to the sick or injured during two world wars.

A tribute to the paid and unpaid nurses from the United Kingdom and the British Commonwealth and Empire, to include the London district nurse killed by bombing on her visits, the fourteen nurses of Salford Royal Infirmary lost in one air raid and the Naval Nursing Sisters all drowned in one boat numbering over forty. One cannot list them all.

OH, WHAT LOVELY BABIES!

GLASGOW ROYAL MATERNITY HOSPITAL, GLASGOW, c. 1920's
A local hospital loved by generations of Glaswegians and known affectionately as Rotten Row
being the name of the street the site is in. Any twins in this bunch? Who owns who? The
doctor to the left of the picture seems very pleased with the production line. Mothers here and
in fact all over the world owe a debt of gratitude to Sir James Young Simpson
of Bathgate, Scotland who discovered Chloroform.
(Courtesy of Glasgow Royal Infirmary)

Oh, what lovely babies!

DISTRICT MIDWIFE/NURSE, FOREST OF DEAN, c. 1905
How is this for transport? Three wheels a little safer than two on skiddy, icy roads. Mrs Grey worked for many years on her district and in those days she was both nurse and midwife to the local community. Other District nurses would apart from using their own feet have the help of a boat, cycle, horse or pony and trap before the advent of the motor car.
Very fond of her trusty tricycle.
(Courtesy of Photocare Laboratories, Kingham)

MEDICAL MISSION AUXILIARY, Church Missionary House, Salisbury Square, London, E.C.

A BATCH OF BABIES IN MENGO HOSPITAL, UGANDA.

A BATCH OF BABIES IN MENGO HOSPITAL, UGANDA
British Midwives seen working in the mission field of Uganda. Held in high esteem for her skill and knowledge and very welcome in any developing country. These midwives look quite hot despite their sun hats. Not an easy option and having to cope with a different, language, a change of climate and many other variations. Snakes, mosquitoes and other unpleasant insects would have caused annoyance.

Oh, what lovely babies!

**PATIENTS ON THE BALCONY OF MARIE CELESTE MATERNITY WARD,
THE LONDON,** 1914
Now known as The Royal London since it's 250th anniversary in 1990. The ward is named
after the wife of a very generous benefactor to the hospital. Edith Cavell (see pp. 66 & 67 'A
Picture of Health') trained to be a nurse at this hospital. These mothers certainly
do not look very happy with their offspring or do they?
(Courtesy of The Royal London Hospital Archives Centre)

TWINS WITH A NURSE,
c. 1910

"With love to my nurse." Twins are always a miracle of birth and the mother will need extra care. The first recorded Caesarian operation in which mother and baby both survived was performed in South Africa by Dr James Barry of The Royal Army Medical Corps in 1820. This brilliant, hard working and well loved Doctor trained at Edinburgh but was really a woman and thus the first woman Doctor (see further reading).

Oh, what lovely babies!

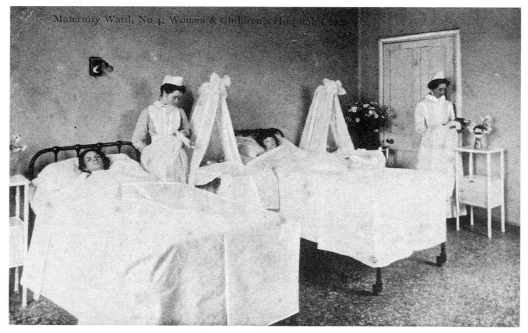

Maternity Ward, No 4. Women & Children's Hospital, Leeds

**WOMEN AND CHILDREN'S HOSPITAL, LEEDS,
MATERNITY WARD NO. 4,** c. 1912

''Dear Eddie, This is where Aunt Mary is now . . .'' A patient or a nurse? Also known as a Lying-in ward because the newly delivered mother in hospital would get a little rest from her usual routine of chores. A mother at home with several children could not lie in for long and had to be soon up and about. Notice the warm canopied cots.

**LITTLE BABY BROTHER
CAME DOWN FROM HEAVEN,
DIDN'T HE NURSE?''**, 1905
One way of looking at it all. How
many readers were told that Stork
brings the baby, it is found under a
mulberry bush (why mulberry I
don't know), or that nurse brings it
in her black bag! How could this
ever be true? The stories many of
us were told . . . As a child I often
wondered how this was in fact
possible.

" *Little baby brother came down from
Heaven, didn't he, nurse?*"
"*Yes, dear.*"
"*I don't blame the angels for chuck-
ing him out—do you, nurse?*"

63

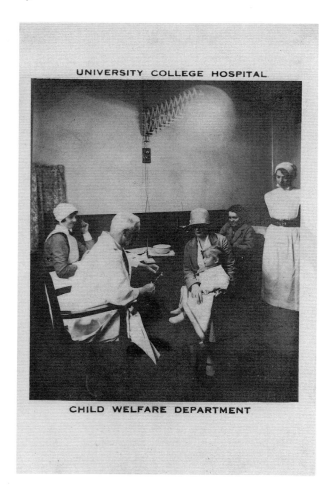

UNIVERSITY COLLEGE HOSPITAL.

CHILD WELFARE DEPARTMENT

CHILD WELFARE DEPT., UNIVERSITY COLLEGE HOSPITAL, c. 1916

For the pre school years the baby growing to childhood could be taken to a local Child Welfare clinic. These clinics were organised in hospitals but usually by the Queen's Nurse of the district and the weekly clinic was held often in a village hall assisted greatly by volunteers. Welfare foods e.g. cod liver oil, orange juice, milk etc., later were sold. The new mother liked to see how her child was progressing and there was also the social side to it with a cup of tea. Imagine the screams as little John is stripped of his clothes and placed on the weighing machine. Quite a noisy afternoon!

CHILDREN SHOULD BE SEEN AND NOT HEARD

GLASGOW ROYAL INFIRMARY, OUT PATIENT'S DEPT., c. 1910
This beautiful old infirmary has a striking facade and inside a most interesting spiral staircase. Lord Lister, Surgeon 1861-1869 was the founder of antiseptic surgery by first using his Carbolic spray, his theory being that germs were in the air. Florence Nightingale and many others scoffed at his ideas however the mortality rate following surgery was drastically cut. A carbolic spray was used on the patient, the operating table, surgeon, and instruments. Patients and surgeons owe much to this persevering Scottish surgeon.
(Courtesy of Glasgow Royal Infirmary)

Christmas, Homœopathic Hospital, Great Ormond Street.

CHRISTMAS, HOMEOPATHIC HOSPITAL, GT. ORMOND ST., c. 1900

Always a lovely time in hospital for the nurses and hopefully for the patients. For weeks before the nurses have been making the decorations as each ward wants to be the best. A tree was given by the local market traders. Christmas Eve the nurses wearing their cloaks inside out to show the red scarlet linings weave in and out of the wards singing carols and carrying lanterns. At some hospitals it was traditional for the carol singing to take place at six o'clock Christmas morning. Patients all wake to find a filled Christmas stocking.

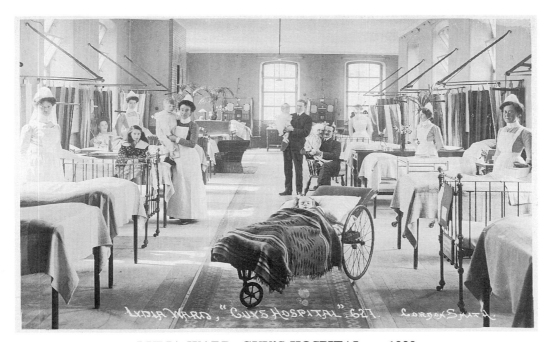

LYDIA WARD, GUY'S HOSPITAL, c. 1900

The world famous Guy's hospital since 1900 has been extensively modernised but a Lydia ward remains. Here children were nursed alongside adults. The child patient seated on a doctor's lap appears to have her right ear bandaged. Possibly suffering the very common and painful condition of the time — Mastoiditis. None of our 90's antibiotics so the disease had to run it's course but sometimes cured by lancing and fomentations. Have Guy's kept the brass plaque as can be seen attached to the cot right hand side of picture?

67

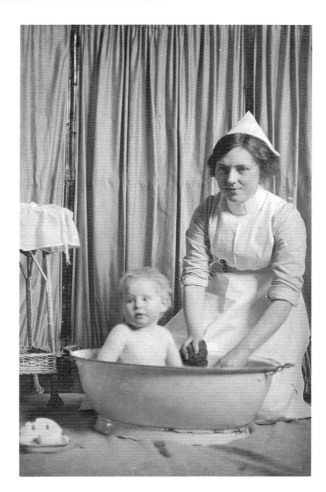

NURSE BATHING A YOUNG PATIENT, LEEDS, c. 1905
Anyone for a bath? Cleanliness is next to Godliness! All children's heads were daily inspected for vermin and many an hour a nurse spent killing nits and lice. Not such an easy job as it looks bathing a child and more difficult still if the child is unwell, wriggling, and crying. This may be the first time the little hospital guest has ever seen such a thing as a bath so it scares him all the more.

Croydon General Hospital, Children's Ward.

CROYDON GENERAL HOSPITAL, CHILDREN'S WARD, c. 1905
What a happy ward scene this is compared to others where toys seem non-existent but woe betide sticky fingers on Sister's highly, daily polished table! The message from the hospital dated 21st October 1917 reads, ''Dear Mrs Cartwright, What has happened to you all on Monday nights, shall be pleased to see you all tomorrow night.
Kind regards to all. F. W. James.''

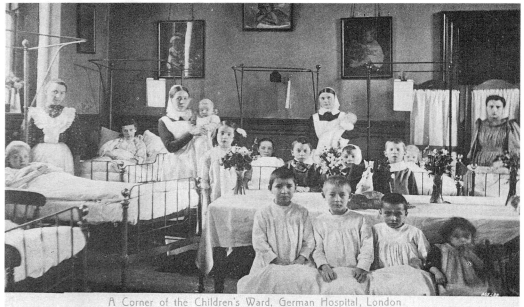

A Corner of the Children's Ward, German Hospital, London

A CORNER OF THE CHILDREN'S WARD, GERMAN HOSPITAL, LONDON

Founded 1845 to care for the German population of London who mostly worked in the sugar factories. Florence Nightingale visited this hospital and was so very impressed by the staff that she then went to Germany to do a three month nurse training with the Kaiserworth nuns. Was it this that decided Miss Nightingale's future? A small hospital with devoted staff that was always open to all and being held in very high esteem by the patients of all nationalities. The closure in 1987 was indeed a sad page of history.

SCHOOL NURSING SERVICE, LIVERPOOL c. 1905
District nursing had it's roots in Liverpool and the valuable School nursing service started in Liverpool. Cuts, boils, a sore foot, inflamed and very paintful ears in they come to see the Queen's Nursing Sister who runs this clinic. Notice the medal worn by the nurse denoting that she is a Queen's nurse. Such was the success of the first clinic for the sick, poor school children of Liverpool that similar clinics were started all over the country.
(Courtesy of National Museums & Galleries of Merseyside)

VICTORIA HOSPITAL, FARQUHAR BALCONY, c. 1905
To get as much sunshine and fresh air as possible balconies like this were attached to many wards of our older hospitals. This is not the Victoria in Scotland. Several hospitals are named after the great Queen Victoria. Can any reader please identify? Notice the Paul cot 1890 to the centre. The very sick looking child to the far right of picture is lovingly surrounded by her toys.

BABIES SUN BATH, LONDON HOSPITAL, c. 1920
Getting better and now able to go for a walk in the hospital grounds. These poor children from London's East end were so in need of sunlight, fresh air and proper food. Dr Barnado founder of the famous Children's homes trained here. The stethescope was pioneered by Dr Thomas Davies 1792-1839 from The London. "Angels of the poor" was the name given to the London Hospital's own visiting Midwives that wore their distinguishing green uniform. Today a few metres from where this picture was taken helicopters land on the roof with seriously ill patients.
(Courtesy of The Royal London Hospital Archives Centre)

Children should be seen and not heard

**SCHOOL MATRON AND
SANATORIUM SISTER,
HEADMASTER AND
TWO PUPILS.
A SCHOOL IN KENT,**
c. 1926

Boys will be boys! Every boarding
school has it's own San, short for
Sanatorium for those that fall sick
or injured and a trained nurse is on
call 24 hours. Measles, football
injuries, cuts and grazes to home
sickness were the order of the day
together with more serious
illnesses. Life had its's funny
moments too as any school
Matron would vouch for.
''Let's play a trick on Matron.''
''No, you do it.''

FLORRIE, SIGNED BY THE AUTHOR, THOS. M. WALKER

Other poems, songs and endless stories have praised the nurse wearing the Red Cross of mercy on her apron. This card cost one penny and "The free proceeds will be handed to the Red Cross and war relief organisations". Rightly described also as "The roses of no man's land". We learn of the thick mud in France during the Great War. Tented hospitals and accommodation for staff including Red Cross nurses were often very muddy and bitterly cold. She performed so many duties that strictly were not her lot but with stretcher upon stretcher of wounded men what else could Florrie say?

"FLORRIE"
(COMPANION TO TOMMY ATKINS).

A Song in Honour of the Red Cross Nurse.
Words by
THOMAS M. WALKER, M.A.
(Govan High School.)

TUNE—TOMMY ATKINS.

She's a modest cultur'd girl with noble aim,
  And she freely leaves her home at Duty's call;
She neither seeks for fortune nor for fame;
  She takes her place while Empires stand or fall,
By Tommy's bed of misery and woe,
  For she knows he guards the home against the foe,
    So she nobly plays her part,
    With a loving cheerful heart;
She's a Florence Nightingale, we'll call her " Flo."

Chorus—
O Florrie, you are Tommy's guardian angel here on earth;
You're the balm for all his sorrows, only Tommy knows your worth,
With your loving heart and tender hand you charm away his woe,
You're sister, wife, and mother all in one, God bless you Flo.

Her graceful figure daintily is clad
  In a uniform, decorous, smart and neat,
And whether she's in cheerful mood or sad,
  Her smiling or her tearful face is sweet;
Yet her charms do no unworthy pride beget,
  That would make her play the role of vain coquette;
    While the Red Cross decks her breast,
    It is Florrie's sole request
To give her life for Tommy without fret.

Chorus—
O Florrie, you are, etc.

She's a heroine in sickness just as true,
  As Tommy is a hero in the trench;
Impartially her duty she will do
  By British, Belgian, German, Turk, or French;
And when War his ghastly course at last has sped,
  And the final drop of human blood has shed,
    Then all true to Nature's plan,
    There's a " soldier and a man "
Who's won sweet Florrie's heart, and whom she'll wed.

Chorus—
O Florrie, you are, etc.

Copyright.

THOS. M. WALKER.

Thomas M Walker

STRETCHER PRACTICE, 1906
Practice makes perfect! Part of any Red Cross training is in carrying the wounded on stretchers but what if there are no proper stretchers available? The nurse learns how to improvise such as the use of a chair or plank of wood. In peace time the invaluable work of the BRCS goes unseen by many except for the clients they seek to help. Luncheon clubs for the elderly and disabled, their visiting service and the loan of medical equipment are much appreciated.
(Courtesy of Nursing Archives of Australia Collection (J.R.W.))

CAMPING, BRCS NURSES, c. 1908
Life under canvas especially a wet, dripping canvas is quite different to a cosy, warm soft bed at home. Even more difficult in the snow and with a fierce gale blowing. Retired VADS have described tents being actually blown away and the mud and the cold ... One needed to be very tough to put up with conditions that no Girl Guide would relish!

INSIDE A MARQUEE, RED CROSS NURSES, c. 1910
Near the battlefield the hospitals were so often tents so we may as well learn how to camp before we go. This picture complete with smart crockery, table cloths, flowers and a finely set table could be lunch at a large fund raising show. Thought to be somewhere in Hove.

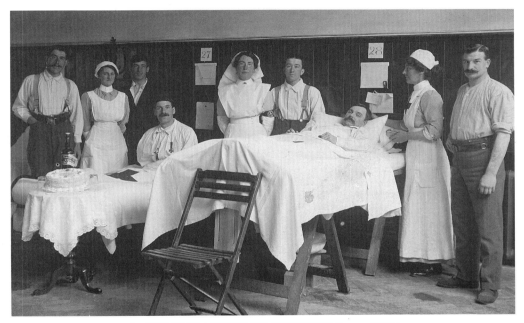

A CELEBRATION IN HOSPITAL, c. 1917
To the left of the picture seated on the bed is an iced cake and a bottle of Old Sherry. The
cake has a Union Jack flag on. The soldier is wearing a medal in the shape of a cross.
Congratulations! Interesting to note is a St. John's nurse to the centre and a Red Cross nurse
at bed 28 clearly showing how the two services worked together for the sick.

SJAB TEAM AND THEIR TROPHY c. 1907

An unknown SJAB team proudly around their hard won challenge cup. Post marked Guildford 1908. What an excellent service this voluntary organisation gives today. At any large public gathering and in all weathers you will see SJAB members ready to offer assistance. Many younger members enter nursing and the Brigade has much to offer to all. The author spent many happy hours as a SJAB cadet. The roller bandaging — a certain skill was really taught to a high standard. We could bandage from head to foot!

JESU, LOVER OF MY SOUL,
1916

One of the many so called Glamour cards churned out in their masses during WWI. In reality as any VAD or nurse will tell you her work is far from glamourous and she was often of more use washing up, cleaning floors or peeling umpteen potatoes. A lot of "Yes, Matron" or "No, Matron". Imagine it so cold at night having to sleep in your clothes and the knives and forks in the mess so cold that they burned your hands. (Tréport, France, winter 1916. See suggested reading.)

JESU, LOVER OF MY SOUL (2).

Other refuge have I none,
  Hangs my helpless soul on Thee;
Leave, ah! leave me not alone,
  Still support and comfort me.
All my trust on Thee is stay'd,
  All my help from Thee I bring;
Cover my defenceless head
  With the shadow of Thy wing.

81

SJAB NURSES, EARLY 1900

Notice the neat little bags hanging from their belts. Each bag contained scissors, thermometer and dressing forceps. Another attachment from the belt carried safety pins. This picture is unidentified. Fully fledged nurses are awarded a brass medal inscribed individually with their name and worn around the neck as can be seen from the card.

SJAB NO. 4, WESTERN DISTRICT

Forever remembered. A tribute to the seventeen Ambulance members and four Nurses all members of SJAB Blackburn, Lancashire who lost their lives 1914-1919 (see p. 56).

BRCS GROUP IN BELGRAVIA WORKROOMS, GROSVENOR CRESCENT, LONDON, c. 1917

Bandages, dressings, and splints being made by Red Cross nurses to the delicate strains of "Oh that we two were marrying". Music helped the hands to work quicker and made for a more pleasant afternoon. These packed supplies of medical needs in addition to being much in demand at home would also be sent to France. A few of the nurses look deep in thought. Perhaps their boy friends are in France?

NOT ALL WORK AND NO PLAY

The Sisters' Gardens.

THE SISTERS' GARDENS, c. 1910

A London photographer but he does not tell us which hospital has such a glorious, sweet scented garden for the sole use of Sisters. Does this haven of peace still exist? Matron sits supreme exempt from any chores. Reminds me of the young medical student who by jumping over the back garden wall was able to get a huge bunch of lovely lilac gathered from Matron's garden to give to his favourite nurse. Although the thief was not caught at eight o'clock next morning nurse was on Matron's mat!

MOST LIKELY TO BE LEEDS ROYAL INFIRMARY NURSES, c. 1905
''My, those skirts and long petticoats will get wet!'' Matron partly in the background seems to
be enjoying it all. In a nurse's short amount of time off in the long day, as little as two hours
this time was meant to ''take exercise'' i.e. not to rest on her bed. As if the nurse didn't get
enough exercise walking up those long wards all day long!

UNKNOWN SCENE, NURSES IN THEIR SITTING ROOM, c. 1916
Time to sew? Stockings to darn and the starched white caps may need sewing to gather in the frills before making up. Splints and many tailed abdominal binders had to be made to perfection ready for the examinations. A television would today take the place of the piano. There is a great collection of piano music in the cupboard. The nurse seated third from the right is knitting socks for her soldier friend in France.

ROYAL EDINBURGH INFIRMARY NURSES, JUNE 1912
What is so very funny here to make these Scottish lassies laugh like this? Quite a change to
see a group of happy, smiling nurses but perhaps the Infirmary was a particularly happy and
friendly place to be? Other cards of REI nurses always show such nice scenes. Maybe the
photographer had a series of exceptional jokes.

ST. MARY'S PADDINGTON, NURSES' SITTING ROOM, 1905

Today one can see a large sign from the motorway coming into London saying "St. Mary's". It was here during WW2 that Sir Alexander Flemming worked for a while on Penicillin, the drug that was about to save countless lives. Typical of any sitting room of the era, although the chairs look a little hard. Notice the tall pot plants and highly polished piano. Staff nurses were afforded a slightly more comfortable room away from the probationers and higher up the hierarchy Sisters had even a little more luxury in their own private domain.

**CORNER OF THE ROOF GARDEN,
ROYAL EAR, NOSE AND THROAT HOSPITAL, SOHO,** c. 1910
More tea! How nurses love their cups of tea. This hospital is now amalgamated with University College. Continues as a small acute hospital of only 39 beds for ear, nose and throat disorders. Up on the roof garden the nurses could get some sunshine and a little rest before returning to the wards.

NURSES HOME HIGHFIELD INFIRMARY.

NURSES' HOME, HIGHFIELD INFIRMARY, 1905

Sent from a nurse in Liverpool, "Here just a week and getting on nicely so far. I was home for an hour or two yesterday evening. Hoping you are well. Yours truly, A. Stowell". The Infirmary and this home now demolished. Difficult windows for a nurse to get into after ten o'clock at night. It was not unheard of for gentleman friends however, to find some hidden entrance to the nurses' home after hours. Love finds a way!

HOSPITAL FOR WOMEN, SHAW ST., LIVERPOOL, c. 1910
Another small hospital having only 59 beds that has managed to escape being gobbled up by the bulldozer. What do you think of their hats? Very much like the domestic servant of the day. Many nurses today choose not to wear the traditional white hats as they associate this with the old domestic servant type image sometimes given to the nurse.

THANK YOU, NURSE

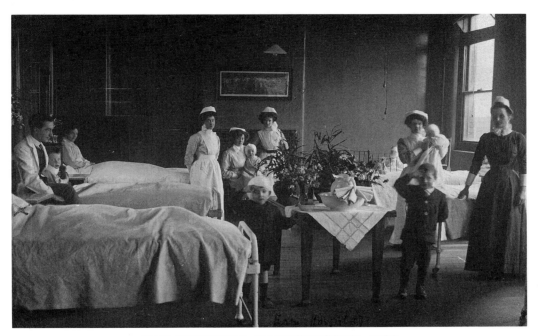

EAR HOSPITAL, MANCHESTER, 1909

Lizzie sends a message, "My dear cousin I am sorry you did not get to see me this morning they only allow one visiting day. The Dr says I am doing nicely but I have a deal of pain in my ear and the dressings are awful." Poor Lizzie she did not exaggerate as ear complaints are indeed painful even with our antibiotics. The x marks Lizzie's bed. How could Sister to the right of the ward breathe wearing such tight 'unmentionables'?

SCOTTISH QUEEN'S NURSES WELCOME THEIR MAJESTIES, c. 1903
Founded in 1889, The Queen Victoria's Jubilee Institute in Edinburgh soon spread all over Scotland. The Sister was sometimes known as a Jubilee nurse. Each Queen's nurse is awarded a bronze medal inscribed with her name and number. The author's own medal is her most prized possession. A gold medal is presented for twenty one years continuous service. Her Royal Highness Princess Alice Duchess of Gloucester is president of The Queen's Nursing Institute, Scotland.

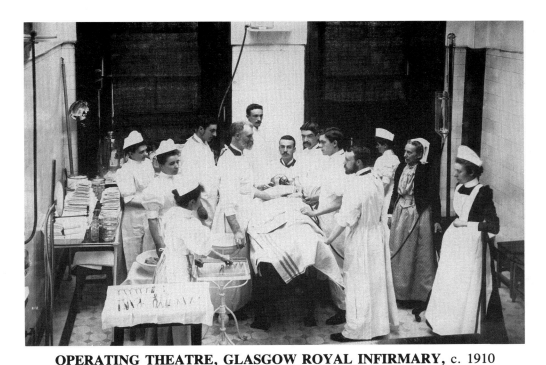

OPERATING THEATRE, GLASGOW ROYAL INFIRMARY, c. 1910
Thank you Lord Lister and to all pioneers and researchers who have made Surgery today so safe. With Lister's carbolic spray the death rate from operations fell from 80% to 50%. At the laying of the foundation stone of this great Infirmary a hymn was sung and part is quoted (author unknown).

''Go bid the spacious dome arise,   Not planned for idle form or show,
And point it's turrets to the skies;   But to alleviate human woe.''
(Courtesy of Glasgow Royal Infirmary)

95

Kent County Ophthalmic & Aural Hospital, The Ophthalmic Consulting Room.

KENT COUNTY OPTHALMIC AND AURAL HOSPITAL,
THE OPTHALMIC CONSULTING ROOM, c. 1925

No patient liked waiting sometimes for hours in an out patient clinic. Long streams of patients got as far as the front door of hospitals as patients prepared to see "The Specialist". They had travelled many miles but in the end it all proves so worthwhile to be given a chance to be seen. Even if no cure or a hopeless case the staff remember "To comfort always". This 96 bedded hospital flourishes, caring for the inhabitants of Kent as the founders wished.

FUNERAL OF A NURSE, EGYPT, 1917
From the message we learn, ''Funeral of a nurse who was killed at a Railway crossing. Unfortunately these sisters' funerals are not that rare owing to the Climate etc.'' Was Sister Anne O'Neill (see 'A Picture of Health', pp. 14, 27 and 79) attending the funeral here of a colleague? So many of the wounded returned home due to the skill and devotion of their nurses.

A QUEEN'S NURSE (UNKNOWN), 1916

''Thank you nurse for bringing my children into the world and helping me when they were sick. You were wonderful when mother died. I will never forget you.'' Through the great generosity of The National Garden's scheme money is raised to help retired Queen's Nurses and younger 'Queenies' who may need assistance by falling on hard times or illness. To all who open their beautiful gardens each year for us — thank you. It is so very appreciated as despite today's welfare services the need for financial assistance is always with us. Notice the Queen's medal and brassard on her left arm.

OPERATING THEATRE, B.G.H.

OPERATING THEATRE, BRISTOL GENERAL HOSPITAL, 1907
No surgeon however skilled could do his work without a nurse's care of the patient before,
during and after the operation. What would the patient do also without the many other hospital
workers that all work to ensure his/her safety and well being? Technicians, cleaners, porters,
laboratory assistants to name just few. Thank you to the numerous voluntary workers attached
to hospitals and The Leagues of Friends. Of great comfort to any hospital are the hospital
chaplains who attend night and day. Notice the anaesthetic trolley and the
weird collection of instruments to right of picture.

GRAVE OF THE LATE MATRON, BUCHANEN HOSPITAL, c. 1908

Goodbye, Matron. Patients remember nurses. Can you remember the nurses that have ever helped you? I can see in my mind's eye so clearly the cheery Queen's nurse who was the school nurse at our local clinic in the late 40's (Shepherd's Bush Rd, London W6). Such a kind nurse and I can't forget her medal on that blue cord. In Manchester Royal Infirmary inscribed in a book of which a page is turned every day are the names of deceased members of the Nurse's league. This book faces the altar of God. May they rest in peace.

AN EASTBOURNE PHOTOGRAPHER, EBU
(On hat badge of a porter)
Looks like all the staff of a small Eastbourne hospital. Who is the young boy? It is nice to see the porters included. Notice the ward maid 3rd row, 1st left, and is that cook 3rd row, 2nd right? The porter is the first person a patient sees as he comes to hospital and the last person to see them as they leave. Hospital porters do a splendid job. At my training school our Head porter at his lodge at the gate knew every nurse as they passed his way under the clock.
Thank you kind porter.

HOSPITAL VISITOR

THE HOSPITAL VISITOR, GLASGOW ROYAL INFIRMARY, c. 1910

The back of the card reads —
"My dear friend I am sending you
a photo of a man
Who goes to the hospital all the
year round to do all the good
he can
Here you will see how he spends
his idle hours
Going to the hospital with books
and flowers
280 of these photos got to be sold
To turn in an extra pound in gold
If all will buy these photos with
a will
The money will go for the hospital
gill (guild)
signed James Hosking. There are
500 female members belonging to
this Guild. Mr. Hosking is the only
gentleman."

(Courtesy of R. Stenlake collection)

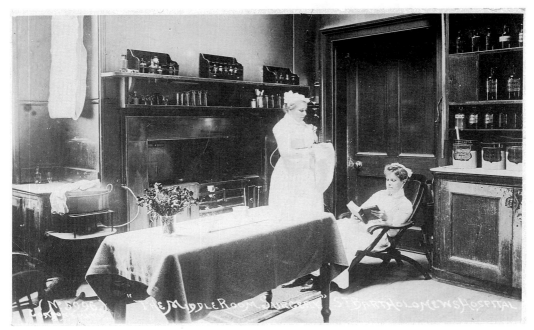

THE MIDDLE ROW SURGERY, ST. BARTHOLOMEW'S HOSPITAL, c. 1900
Nurse Birch is seen standing and seated is Nurse Senior. The message is especially interesting.
''The immortal Middle Room in the old surgery where cocoa is provided for all comers at 12
mn and 2 am and where teeth are drawn daily.'' Hospital nights are always long, and
frequently cold as the silver moon peers into the wards. Thank you nurse
for watching over and nursing us at night.

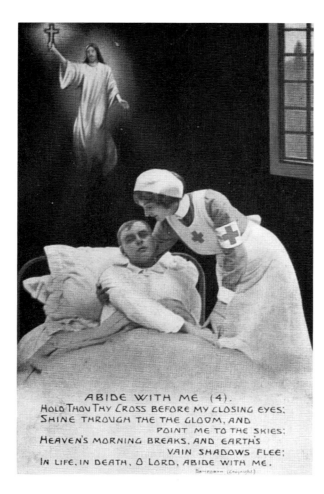

ABIDE WITH ME (4).
HOLD THOU THY CROSS BEFORE MY CLOSING EYES;
SHINE THROUGH THE THE GLOOM, AND
POINT ME TO THE SKIES;
HEAVEN'S MORNING BREAKS, AND EARTH'S
VAIN SHADOWS FLEE;
IN LIFE, IN DEATH, O LORD, ABIDE WITH ME.

ABIDE WITH ME, c. 1915
The author having been a patient several times in various hospitals has just reason to say, "THANK YOU NURSE". Prayer of St. Augustine from a card bought at Leicester Royal Infirmary chapel. "Watch thou, dear Lord, with those whom wake, or weep tonight and give thine Angels charge over those who sleep. Tend thy sick ones, O Lord Christ. Rest thy weary ones. Bless thy dying ones. Soothe thy suffering ones. Pity thine afflicted ones. And all for thy love's sake."

INDEX

INDEX CONTINUED